GUIDE TO
A DOCKLAND
OF CHANGE

GUIDE TO
A DOCKLAND
OF CHANGE

A PRESENT DAY, HISTORICAL,
ANECDOTAL AND (1949-1969) PHOTOGRAPHIC GUIDE TO
THE RIVERSIDE DOCKS AND WHARVES BETWEEN
THE TOWER OF LONDON AND LIMEHOUSE

Written and photographed by
JAMES PAGE-ROBERTS

The Mudlark Press

British Library Cataloguing-in-publication data

A catalogue record for this book is available from the British Library

First published in 1997 by The Mudlark Press
PO Box 13729, London W6 9GN

Copyright © James Page-Roberts June 1997

Photographs and maps copyright © James Page-Roberts

All rights reserved, including the right of reproduction in whole or in part in any form

Design and typeset by Ray Leaning

Printed and bound   by Biddles, Guildford, Surrey.

Cover design by Robert Page-Roberts

ISBN 0 9530517 0 6

CONTENTS

I would like to thank the Port of London Authority for so generously allowing me access to the docks, all those who tested the guide for me, and George L. Saunders, of the Company of Watermen and Lightermen of the River Thames, for verifying my dockside terms and jargon.

I dedicate this book to Margreet.

Books also written by the author include:
VINES IN YOUR GARDEN (Argus Books),
THE BEST WINE IN THE SUPER MARKET (Foulsham),
The first three editions of
THE BEST WINE BUYS IN THE HIGH STREET (Foulsham),
THE OLDIE COOKBOOK (Carbery Press),
VINES AND WINES IN A SMALL GARDEN (Herbert Press),
WINES FROM A SMALL GARDEN (Abbeville Press, New York)
DRUIF EN WIJN UIT EIGEN TUIN (Schuyt, Haarlem).

PREAMBLE

The smell of exotic spices, the dense pea-soup fogs that blanketed sight and muffled the sound of barges in chain harness, the occasional rat going about its business, the ill odours of pollution rising from murky tidal water, the cheeriness and friendliness of those who worked there... What was it that drew me back to docklands so often and for so long?

Perhaps I first became aware of the district as a young and proud trainee RAF pilot when Nazi bombs seemed to be especially directed at that part of London. Or was it when I mended bomb-shattered roofs as a slater in the East End while waiting to gain my wings in the bright air of Oklahoma? Perhaps it was as a TB convalescent. Or was it as a medical student, or perhaps as a matelot supernumerary walking from Custom House in Billingsgate to Dundee Wharf in Limehouse to board ship? But whenever venturing into that supposedly sleazy, dockland part of the great capital, I became completely enthralled by what I saw and felt. I was to return time and time again, and to love it enough to build a house there so that I could live in one of its busiest parts.

A feeling of age pervaded the place in those days. Wharves and warehouses, flattened by the explosions of war, created a neglected, run-down air. Grasses and buddleia sprouted from the ruins. A busy and vibrant world in daylight, it became silent, desolate and slightly sinister by night.

To anyone who did not live or work in docklands it was an unvisited, unknown quarter. This was the small, tight world that was to help form my life from shortly after the conclusion of wartime hostilities until twenty years or so later. It was to be the inspiration for my photographs, paintings and sculpture.

Then I neglected the area, moving away to America, rather as the Virginia Settlers had done before me. But I never forgot it. Now the place has changed out of all recognition. Gone is the daytime bustle and noise, lost are the delicious and noxious smells, disappeared are the craftsmen and artisans who inhabited the sheds and archways of yore and who could make or mend almost anything for you. Dockland has become a domestic and office world, and an ever-changing one, new, bright and clean.

Let us go there now together to look at it, recall the recent and distant past in words and photographs, and speculate on its future.

THE HISTORY

Although the docks in London present the appearance of great age, their development, in terms of England's history, is comparatively recent. So to see how the wharves and docks came about, let us go right back to when primitive man, woman and beast found a ford, or causeway, to cross to the other side of the river Thames. This crossing place, at low tide, was near to the Westminster Bridge of today.

A bridge, constructed close to the present London Bridge, was known to be in existence by AD 43. The site had been chosen because there was a steep rise of gravel on either shore.

To the east of it, where now stands the Tower of London, was an area of high ground, free from flooding, and ideal for fortification. Nearby there were tributaries of clear, clean water entering the Thames. Of these, the Walbrook, and perhaps the Fleet, were already in use as a safe anchorage for vessels.

So the natural geographical advantages of this part of England were ideal for the establishment of a successful military and trading base.

Its very early history can only be surmised. But through Stone, Bronze, and Iron Ages, the conglomeration of houses, businesses and wharfage could only grow in importance.

When the Romans arrived, they found trade flourishing on the reinforced river bank and a busy economy at work.

As a military base this place commanded great tracts of country to the north and south. And where tidal water narrowed from its wide, sluggish, estuarine state to become a strong, concentrated, deep and scouring flow, the position became, quite naturally, the centre of commerce and power.

Early imports were ivory, necklaces, glass, pottery and amber, with exports of slaves, corn, live animals, hides, dogs, iron, tin, lead and gold.

With the Romans encamped, and law and order under their control, London became the hub for both national and international trade. Fostered by a highly efficient administration, and protected by a powerful army of occupation, its trading boundaries now became those of the mighty Roman Empire.

Invasion by commercial immigrants, and inter-marriage, produced a polyglot race of Londoners. These mongrels were strong and hard-working. They had to be - or perish.

Everything was now in favour of London, bridged across the Thames, becoming one of the greatest cities in the world - despite the incendiary attentions of such as Boadicea.

Then the Romans departed. And without their powerful presence, anarchy prevailed.

But Saxon London and its people were survivors. With a leftover Roman or two, no doubt, it was soon to suffer from the rapacity of conquering Danes and Norwegians. Londoners absorbed their bloodlines in turn - sometimes, no doubt, involuntarily.

Rulers rose and fell. Londoners worked hard and prospered.

In the days of King Canute, London was the headquarters of the Navy and the chief centre for the building of merchantmen and men-of-war.

Then the Normans took over and, in their turn, were assimilated. Their culture fed the minds of our countrymen. Their military might held control.

Now, with a continental ruler on the throne, trade across the Channel flourished. Merchants from Normandy, Flanders, Italy, Spain and elsewhere, settled in the increasingly important city. Wine merchants from France set up shop. The wool trade prospered as never before. And with all this wealth, London's businessmen became a powerful force in the land - and the world.

The Middle Ages were a fruitful period of exploration and power. Henry VII was a business monarch. Henry VIII opened up trade with Russia. The East India Company was founded. And in the reign of Elizabeth I, many successful treasure hunting expeditions took place. By obtaining the freedom of the seas after the defeat of the Spanish Armada, the world's trading routes and markets were now open to a business community that proceeded, once more, to turn London into the commercial centre of the world.

Eastern spices and artefacts, wines, furs, fish, coal, hops, ale, ordinance, saffron, timber, pelts, cheese, drapery, tobacco, cattle... London traded in them all - and more.

A plague, the Dutch blockade, a sweeping fire, repeated intrusions by the Dutch fleet... what of them? Londoners were resilient, imaginative, creative - and mercenary.

All this trading of goods took place in the very heart of the metropolis - with the help of a strong, six-hourly tide that swept in ships on the ebb from all quarters, and out with the flow. This natural movement of water was a free and enduring source of motive power for vessels that otherwise relied on wind and oar for propulsion.

At the waterside quays and river moorings there now flourished a great deal of theft and dealing in contraband. So one might imagine that an inland dock, well walled, would have been constructed to offer security from the villains. But the first dock, the Howland, in Rotherhithe, completed sometime after 1696, is depicted in contemporary illustrations as having no protection other than several rows of rather elegant, deciduous trees. The dock's purpose was to be a quiet haven for up to 120 of the largest merchant ships afloat. The advantages offered were that the vessels and their sailors would be shielded from the difficulties encountered in bad weather and on tidal water - a benefit demonstrated when, in the great storm of 1703, only one ship in the dock suffered damage, when most of those in the river were torn from, or dragged their moorings, to founder on the north shore. So, in that respect, the dock was a success.

Even the next dock to be constructed, the equally tree-lined Brunswick (1789), was only for the fitting out and repairing of ships - its mast tower being a prominent feature.

Both also gave protection from the destructive power of fast moving river ice and, by providing cook rooms ashore, were able to save the wooden vessels from the ever-present hazard of being burnt to the water line.

The 18th century was one of wars and commercial stagnation - until Clive's campaigns in India engendered trade with the East. Coupled with the burgeoning West Indian sugar and rum trade, London once more became a prosperous city.

Then, West India merchants, fed up with the disruptions to their trade by the thieving activities of thousands of riverside and waterborne pirates on the over-congested river (the thieves were even known by their specialist activities - River Pirates, Night Plunderers, Light Horsemen, Heavy Horsemen, Scuffle-Hunters and Mud Larks, etc.), decided to found the wall-protected West India Dock in a marshy Thames oxbow known as the Isle of Dogs.

So, in 1802, the advantages of enclosed docks became realised. Soon to follow West India Dock was London Dock (1805). This was dug from the north bank of the river near to the Tower of London. After that, the less successful St. Katherine Dock was squeezed in between it and the Tower in 1828. So in historical terms, the docks, as such, are a comparatively recent manifestation, though the wharfage is as old as London's original inhabitants.

What happened to it all? In 1967 (the period of the photographs) there were some 67,000 dockers at work. Then, although small containers had been in use at such as Irongate Wharf in the late 1930s, goods on pallets and in much larger containers bypassed the out of date and expensive wharves. By 1972 there were only 15,000 dockers working, and those mostly in the large docks downriver. The decline had been sudden.

THE PHOTOGRAPHS

The photographs in this guide were taken from "the road" between 1949 and 1969. They were never meant to be a record of the district, only a guide to help me see dockland in form and related shapes. It is quite by chance that they have become of historic interest.

It was sheer luck that in 1969 I set some aside as a memento of my life in dockland. With negatives long ago destroyed, I discovered the photographs shown here when furniture was recovered from storage some time in the late 1980s.

The cameras that recorded these scenes in black and white were a series of Baby Brownies, one box, one Bakelite, and another, mended with passe-partout and India ink. They were almost as unsophisticated as cameras could be - to our present-day way of thinking. But they recorded as I peered through their flip-up aiming devices, "clicked", and wound on film.

THE GUIDE

W hether on foot, bicycle, in a wheelchair, or even tucked up in an armchair or bed, we start this guide to a magical stretch of London's dockland at Tower Bridge and end it in Limehouse.

If on foot, depending upon your speed and the number of detours, refreshments and rests taken, allow 4 hours, give or take, from start to finish. I have done it briskly and without detours in 1 1/2 hours. The total mileage from start to finish point, without diversions, is about 4 3/4 miles (7.6 km). This is quite a long way for those unused to walking. So you might like to interrupt the journey by having a picnic overlooking the river, or lunch and a drink or two at one of the several riverside pubs. On the other hand, if you are short of time or breath, you could break off the journey part way at Wapping Underground Station, 1 1/2 miles (2.4 km) down the road. Here you could turn back, having had a good sight and feel of dockland. Or, from this point you could take the tube to Whitechapel and there change on to the District Line back. Also, from immediately outside the station, the 100 bus, coming every 15 minutes, will return you to Aldgate and the City. Week-end public transport services are not as frequent as during the week.

Taking this walk at low water, or near to it, will enable you to reach the river shore by the several "stairs" (more on these later). Take a chance (tides turn about every six hours), or check the tide tables in a quality newspaper.

Go prepared for the weather. Wrap up well when it is cold, and pay regard to forecasts in the newspapers and on radio and television.

Sometimes gates close off the THAMES PATH in the evening. They may appear to be closed in daytime. Do not be deterred. Push or pull them to gain access. The same applies to the gates that guard stairs.

To reach the starting place of our walk it would be wise first to buy an all-day ticket for unlimited travel by bus and Underground (from 09.30 until midnight). With this, alight at TOWER HILL Underground Station (District Line). Face the Tower of London, take a little kink to the left and right, and walk down steps and through the pedestrian underpass in front of you.

Now turn either to the right or left. To the *right* you follow the path around the Tower (with handy public conveniences on your right hand). Walk along by the river, the Upper Pool, and take the arch beneath Tower Bridge and turn right to the river again. This route is about 1/4 mile (0.4 km) in length.

Should you turn *left*, take the tunnel beneath Tower Bridge Road, turn right, and follow the THAMES PATH to the river, keeping St. Katherine Dock and the amphitheatre on your left. This way is shorter.

By either route, you are now on the river wharf where several old mooring bollards for the ships at Irongate Wharf remain. Boules is played on a gravelly quay.

Carry on close to the river, if the boules surface is not too wet and sticky, passing the modern St. Katherine Pier on the right and the Tower Thistle Hotel on the left. Cross the pedestrian bridge at the St. Katherine Dock entrance, where boats enter or leave when the tide is high, and look back toward Tower Bridge (photograph No.1).

Notes on photograph No.1:

The cranes are on St. Katherine and Irongate Wharves. The warehouses (where The Tower Thistle Hotel now stands) held general cargo and bonded wines and spirits. Once passengers sailed from St. Katherine Wharf to the ports of Europe.

The photograph was taken from the eastern knuckle of the

dock entrance, using the cracks between the then wooden boards to direct the eye toward the coaster being loaded or off-loaded at St. Katherine Wharf.

The barges across the river are moored at Battle Bridge Tier (a tier is a fixed mooring to fore and aft buoys for ships or barges). The ocean-going vessel beyond is tied up to Hay's (the larder of London), Humphrey's, Cotton's or Chamberlain's Wharves.

The taller bollard on the far knuckle will almost certainly have been a captured cannon from the Napoleonic wars, embedded in concrete. These guns made excellent bollards, beside being useful reminders to those who used them of the might of the British Navy. Each was filled with sand or concrete and had a cannon ball lodged in the barrel mouth.

Carry on, taking note of the Dockmaster's House (1830) immediately on the right and St. Katherine Dock in front of you. Take the THAMES PATH alleyway to the right and, when at the brick road, ST. KATHERINE'S WAY, look back toward the Dockmaster's House. From close by, photograph No.2 was taken in the years after the war when reconstruction after the damage, inflicted by German bombs, had yet to be undertaken.

Notes on photograph No.2:

This photograph of a part of Tower Bridge and a wall of corrugated iron was taken from near the Dockmaster's House. The warning notice related to the weight limit when using the St. Katherine Dock Entrance bridge.

Fortuitous or not, the four lamps were each given a setting of their own.

Now you can either continue walking down St. Katherine's Way, or take a most pleasing detour by turning left up a slope to investigate the St. Katherine Dock complex of modern and sympathetically converted warehouses in their water setting.

With firing from a battery of guns from the eastern quay of Eastern Dock, and with the entry of two three-masted sailing ships dressed overall, and with their sailors thick on the yards, St. Katherine Dock, consisting of the Basin and Eastern and Western Dock, was opened in October 1828. But even with its warehouses full of wool, ivory, indigo, tea, shells and scents, it was never a commercial success - unlike now. Of the original buildings only two remain. These are the Ivory House (formerly "I" warehouse that specialised in the handling of ivory, scent and shells) in the middle with its bell tower, and the Dockmaster's House.

Fortify yourself, if you will, with coffee, tea, or stronger drink at the Dickens Inn or any of the other eating and drinking places that are there. Return to the dockland road (ST. KATHERINE'S WAY), turn left, and continue toward Limehouse.

Almost immediately you will see the offices of Devon House on the right. This building stands on the site of British and Commonwealth Wharf and South Devon Wharf (photograph No.3).

Notes on photograph No.3:

This photograph of a security fence outside the wharves, looked over a bombed site toward a crane operating on South Devon Wharf. I thought it to be a pleasant arrangement made from bleak and forbidding ingredients. The wharf once handled tea and wool. But of more interest now is that some of the structure of Dickens Inn (which you may have visited in St. Katherine Dock) came from a brewery warehouse on this site.

Walk on past President's Quay House, President Quay and HMS President, then, very soon, down the side of Millers Wharf, comes the first of the stairs - Alderman Stairs. When the river was full of shipping, which was probably from before Roman times until the advent, and beyond, of enclosed docks (which were built for protection of shipping from the elements and goods from the thieves), these stairs allowed those wanting to reach the moored vessels in the river to descend from the river bank to hire or take a rowing boat to their destination. The unwary were then sometimes in the hands of villains. Thomas Rowlandson depicts it beautifully in 1818, describing his engraving of the scene as: Passengers being assailed by a group of watermen holding up their hands and bawling out "Oars Sculls. Sculls. Oars Oars". Then, as now, these stairs can be slippery, especially around the high water level. So be very careful when using them.

Look to the left to see the remains of the jetty at Carron Wharf, behind which the modern Summit building now stands. Across the river is Butler's Wharf and the Design Museum. On the right you will see HMS President, the Royal Navy Reserve's President Quay, and Tower Bridge.

When the river was busy with commerce, a great deal of flotsam and jetsam floated with the wind and tide to rest on the river gravel or mud (photograph No.4)

Notes on photograph No.4:

This hand-cart wheel, the steel cable, can and manila rope, were typical of the objects to be seen on the muddy shore of the river when the tide was out. If you were able to see through the squalor, there were pleasant patterns to be found. There still are. Surprisingly, at the bottom of Alderman Stairs are probably the very same steel cables seen protruding from the mud in the photograph taken 40 or more years ago.

Return to your route along ST. KATHERINE'S WAY and almost immediately, on the other side of the modern Summit office building, take a turn right to the THAMES PATH and walk beside the river in front of Tower Bridge Wharf. This will lead you to the filled-in Hermitage Entrance to London Dock. The entrance was opened into the basin and dock in 1821. Made for small vessels and barges, it was closed in 1909 (photograph No.5).

Notes on photograph No.5:

This photograph was taken from the road that crosses the

closed Hermitage Entrance to London Dock. Note the depth
gauge carved into the stonework in Roman numerals.

The lower curve was made to accommodate the bulbous
bottoms of wooden sailing ships - there being virtually no steam
at the time of its construction (the first steamship arrived in the
Thames in 1815). With the advent of steam and strength of steel,
the bottoms of trading vessels were squared off to accommodate
more cargo and allow stable rest on mud or gravel. This new
shape made the curved entrance quite unsuitable.

The barge, resting on its campshed, was in for repair at the
Badger Engineering and Repair yard immediately to the right. (A
campshed is a raised berth, enclosed by a low row of pilings on
the foreshore, visible at low water. It served the purposes of
allowing a barge to tie up close to the quayside without canting
over on a sloping shore at low water, preventing a heavy barge
from sliding away with its moorings on sloping mud, and to level
the cargo. The best had a top layer of chalk They are also known
as barge beds.)

Regain ST. KATHERINE'S WAY and directly in front of you is poorly
marked THOMAS MORE STREET. Take it, pausing to look into
Hermitage Basin on the right (photograph No.6) and at the elegant wall
leading up and away to London Dock, Gate 24.

Notes on photograph No.6:

This view, looking over Hermitage Basin into Western Dock
of London Dock, is seen through a Catherine wheel shaped
railing. The capped dock wall (1802-1805) that soars away to
the right is, gratefully, still there.

The crane in the left middle distance was powered by pressure
from the London Hydraulic Company's Pumping Station near to
the entrance to Shadwell Basin (we pass it later). It was the only
crane of its kind in the Western Dock. The cranes in the distance
were working on the northern quay of Western Dock. Photograph
No.7 was taken from the warehouse beyond the bollard.

Note the remains of fascist graffiti on the foreground wall.

Some observers fancifully believe that the capitals of Dock Gate 25, in front of you, depict elephants beneath jungle trees. The decoration on other gate capitals in London Dock rather discount this.

Keeping Hermitage Basin on your right, and just before the second bend in THOMAS MORE STREET, note Quay 430 ahead and beyond it the top of News International headquarters. Immediately behind a glass-bricked block of flats on the left, in the huge, white stone and glass complex of Thomas More Square, is an extensive Safeway supermarket (where you might buy picnic food and drink).

You now reach VAUGHAN WAY. Turn right and pause to glance left along Spirit Quay at the channel where Western dock was once located. Beyond is Cesar Pelli's tower at Canary Wharf. Now turn right to walk along the side of Hermitage Basin. And as you do so, look at the powerful side walls of the defunct lock between basin and dock (photograph No.7).

Notes on photograph No.7:

This was taken from Hermitage Basin through X Warehouse toward 9 Shed with its step-back. The channel and lock leading from the Basin to Western Dock is guarded by the chain seen on the right. The Western Dock and the warehouse land beyond now supports housing.

Within the docks and not far away to the north, stood, for me, the magical Crescent Wine Vaults. Below ground there was an enormous area of stored wine in casks resting under a low roof of brick arches thickly hung with edible fungus. Supposedly built by Napoleonic prisoners of war, this dimly lit and almost silent underground world was kept at a constant temperature by a few naked gas lamps. It was necessary for the coopers in charge of wines to sample casks on a regular basis to ensure that the claret, Burgundy, Italian wine, sherry, port and the rest remained in good condition. To a man they favoured sweet wine, so my advice was often sought on the drier ones - with sometimes staggering results. The casks were opened by hitting the staves on either side of the shive (bung) with a flogger (a wedge-headed mallet with a long handle). Into the wine went a large valinche (pipette) made of tin. A thumb then covered the air vent at the top of the valinche, the instrument was extracted from the barrel, off came the thumb and the wine, held in the valinche until then by suction, was run into glasses - invariably with their broken stems set into cork bungs. Should a wine be cloudy or turning to vinegar, there was a resident wine chemist in the docks who could convert almost any cask of "off" wine into something drinkable.

Return toward the river, and the road (that was St. Katherine's Way and has now become the poorly marked WAPPING HIGH STREET), continuing along the quayside, keeping Hermitage Basin on your right. Exit through the large gateway (formerly Gate 24), taking note of the Pumping Station building to your right, dated 1914. This was built to replenish dock water after the Hermitage Entrance was closed (to tidal water as well as shipping).

A tidal mill (Crash Mills) had been established here in medieval days. As the tide rose in the river, water would rush into the mill pond (more or less Hermitage Basin) through a sluice. The sluice would be closed at high water, the tide fell in the river, and the pond emptied through rotating paddle wheels to turn grain into flour between millstones.

After leaving the dock gate, turn immediately almost back on yourself to the left into REDMEAD LANE, keeping the Scots Arms and China Ship pubs on your right hand side. To the left stood the enormous Hermitage Wall and its continuation guarding the bottling and other warehouses of London Dock. Do not dwell here for long as there is nothing to show what the walls were like, except by referring to photograph Nos.8-12. As you see, this was a rather neglected backwater.

Notes on photograph Nos.8-12:
Photograph No.8.

The gas street lamp had by then been converted to electricity. The massive Hermitage Wall was made of London Stock bricks, and the mortar old and weak, So when the walls were torn down at the end of the life of London Dock, many bricks were recovered and used again in the reconstruction of the district. A mellow brick of pale golden yellow to reddish, the gradations of "stock", "second hard" or "hard" (well baked), all gain mellowness with age.

Photograph No.9.

In the way that dockers walk, this one was passing the simply designed concrete lamp posts and a Winston Churchill election poster on his way to the China Ship pub for a pint. We glance at the activity in Western Dock.

Photograph No.10.

We are looking back toward Tower Bridge, where refuse, a water stop-cock being turned by an official, and the ever-present walls of dockland, lead the eye forward to cranes and Tower Bridge.

Photograph No.11.

Dockland could be bleak on a rainy day. The eye is led over wet cobblestones toward Tower Bridge from Redmead Lane.

Photograph No.12.

This photograph of a figure, set in a street of cobbles and brick walls, leads the eye past him and over warehouses beside Wapping Basin to the trees beyond in Wapping Gardens.

After you have walked just a little up Redmead Lane, trying to absorb the atmosphere of walls and cobbles of old, turn back toward Wapping High Street, now keeping the China Ship and Scots Arms on your left. Turn left around the Scots Arms into WAPPING HIGH STREET. A few paces along and on your right stood the massive Colonial and Globe Wharves (photograph No.13).

Notes on photograph No.13:

The doorstep of this opening in the roadside wall of Colonial Wharf must have been at one time the lintel of a street level light or ventilation window. Anyhow, during the life of the now non-existent building, a narrow door-opening was needed. A new lintel was inserted and glazed bricks used to surround the doorway. Judging by the scrape marks, the height was determined by that of the load-carrying surface of carts and trucks. But how was a docker to climb in and out? Simple. Hack out some footholds.

The "safe load" notice referred to the warehouse crane above.

The roadsides of these warehouses were often dull to look at. From the river side, on the other hand, the architecture was more elaborate. Photograph Nos.14-16 will give an idea of this.

Notes on photograph Nos.14-16:
Photograph No.14.

The newer part of the warehouse to the right of Colonial Wharf was at that time under construction. A crane had yet to be added. This wharf and warehouse aspect was typical of the river frontage in the 1950s days of high activity. The photograph shows bulk, power and elegance, set off by the dented foreground barge resting on the campshed .

Photograph No.15.

Barges resting on the campshed, warehouses, and a "preying mantis" of a crane on its jetty with Tower Bridge in the background, were seen at low tide from near Union Stairs and Causeway, next to Colonial and Globe Wharves. The rope under tension draws the foreground together to accentuate the shape of the cranes (there are two - one behind the other).

Photograph No.16.

The bulkiness of these barges, moored to Colonial Wharf on the campshed and shore, is illustrated by the relatively small size of the lighterman (the elite of river workers) walking along the deck of his barge nearest to the warehouse. His barge rests on the campshed.

That there were frequent drownings in the river is quite within one's comprehension when considering the speed and fury of the tidal current and the weight and ferocity of the clashing together of the barges in turbulent water. The bows, called "swims" were almost shaped especially to suck the unwary beneath them with the tide. If unfortunate enough to go this way, it was advisable to raise an arm on reaching the stern to prevent yourself from hitting the fixed rudder, the "budget plate". The photograph gives a sense of this awesome power.

A little further along WAPPING HIGH STREET, Union Stairs (sometimes inaccessible) lead down to the river. Although we will pass Execution Dock (or rather where it stood) later, this photograph (No.17), with its hanging rope where children played at low tide, gives a good feeling of the summary justice meted out to any malefactor caught in the more brutal and callous days of the past.

Notes on photograph No.17:

Beyond this evocative scene at Union Stairs, and on the other bank of the river beyond a barge on the shore, is Tower Bridge Wharf, just beyond the Victorian confection of Tower Bridge. Here, hides were imported to supply the local leather industry.

Back on our route, look forward along this straight stretch of WAPPING HIGH STREET to the bend. There you will see part of some houses at the Wapping Entrance to London Dock. But before you reach there, just before the turning left into Sampson Street, and on the ground where Zanzibar and Fuchsia Court now lie, once stood a spice warehouse. So steeped was the fabric of this building with the smell of pepper and other spices that for many years after it was demolished the rubble emitted fragrance that bathed the air around. You may still sense it - even if only in your imagination. Such were the smells of dockland that lightermen and tugmen could locate themselves on the river at night or in fog by the smells of warehouses containing spice, fruit, wine, skins, ginger, tea, nuts, oils, hops and suchlike.

After Capital Wharf we now reach the Wapping Entrance to London Dock with its handsome Pierhead terraced houses on either side. They were built between 1810 and 1813 for officials of London Dock. The entrance, with the lock sides preserved, was closed in the early 1960s, leaving the Shadwell Entrance as the only usable one for London Dock. This complex of docks had now become an enormous storage area for wool, ivory, rubber, wine, spirits, spices and much more. Look at the lock entrance gates with their worn capitals and bases (trunks, possibly, but not elephants this time) and beyond at the tower of St. George's-in-the-East, a Hawksmoor church (see information later about St. Anne's).

Continuing, we come to the Town of Ramsgate pub on the right with Wapping Old Stairs running down to the water beside it. This is where Thomas Rowlandson drew passengers being harried by watermen in the early part of the 19th century.

There are many stories about this pub and its association with the infamous Judge Jeffreys. A good judge in his early career, he acquired a bad name in 1685 at the "bloody assizes" in Winchester, when he sent 320 people to the gallows and hundreds to be transported or sold into slavery after Monmouth failed in his uprising against James II. This aristocratic Baron/Judge shared the callous attitudes of his time to the lower classes and villains in general. A supporter of Catholic James II, who, when the king was forced to flee on the approach of William of Orange, tried the same without success. Some say that he was apprehended in the pub itself, asleep, dressed as a woman, or as a sailor with cut-off eyebrows. Others believe that he was caught at Wapping New Stairs (we see them later) about to board ship, when he was betrayed by someone he had punished and taken to another inn, the Red Cow in no longer existent Anchor and Hope Alley (which led to Broad Street where Captain Bligh was later to own a house). Anyhow, he was dragged to the Tower of London, where he died in considerable pain from the "stones" (gall or kidney, presumably) - a condition that some think may well have caused him to be so cruel and severe during the latter part of his life.

Oliver's Wharf, next door, was one of the first river warehouses to be converted to living accommodation. This fine Victorian building is more gracious when seen from the river side. Then comes Orient Wharf (photograph No.18).

Notes on photograph No.18:

The ground mooring chains that secured barges off Orient Wharf await the arrival of tidal water. Then, especially when the wash from a passing ship or tug would strike, there would be a mighty clanging and rattling of chains. Noises such as these were a constant reminder that the river, when unseen from the roadway, was nearby.

On the other side of the road from Oliver's and Orient Wharves, and by the side of SCANDRETT STREET, stands an unusually shaped area of grass, being the old graveyard for the church of St. John, of which only the tower now stands after German bombing. Next to it is St. John of Wapping School, founded in 1695 (about Judge Jeffrey's time). Painted figures of a boy and a girl, dressed in contemporary style, have a niche apiece - schooling then being very much segregated.

An optional quick detour down SCANDRETT STREET to TENCH STREET will show tall, mottled and repaired dock walls on the left, Wapping Gardens on the right, and 22 Gate leading to the old Eastern Dock of London Dock. Only if you are interested in Captain Bligh, of the Bounty and mutiny, continue into Reardon Street, which was Broad Street in his day, keeping the old dock wall on your left. There you will see a plaque on a wall marking where he lived in the latter part of the 18th century.

Returning to WAPPING HIGH STREET, again at Pierhead Wharf, and crossing over to the riverside pavement, you will notice that the set of the two Orient Wharf buildings change in their frontage line - one part jutting more into the pavement. This is where photograph No.19 was taken.

Notes on photograph No.19
This plaque was affixed to a warehouse wall that intruded upon the pavement of Wapping High Street, close to what is now Toynbee Housing Association Shared Ownership Flats, Orient Wharf. The plaque had been destroyed before I left the district in 1969.

Catwalk conveyors between warehouses are still there, but beyond, between Dundee Court (St. John' s Wharf Warehouse of old) and St. Thomas's Wharf.

Pass under the two catwalks, walkways or flying bridges (more on these later) that span the road and, just after the mould-fronted Metropolitan Police Boatyard (where launches are raised up from the water by lift for repair), turn right into a small and pleasant park with Wapping New Stairs (probably where Judge Jeffreys *was* caught) in the far corner. Take a rest, and possibly enjoy your picnic, as you look at the river, and across it to the Angel pub (of 15th century origin and frequented by Samuel Pepys and Turner, etc.) and to its left, St. Mary's church and Canary Wharf. Just downstream is the Police Pier.

Now, continuing along WAPPING HIGH STREET, you come to the Police Station (photograph No.20) and Metropolitan Police Thames Division Headquarters, with the unmarked Wapping Police Stairs down the side of the building between the Station and Old Aberdeen Wharf. Here, at low water, are several signs of old river wharfage and a "grid" on which police launches could lie for inspection or repair. These are excellent stairs from which to climb down to the river bed.

Look across the river and slightly to the left to see the church steeple of St. Mary's, Rotherhithe. Here Captain Christopher Jones of the Mayflower lies buried (1662).

Notes on photograph No.20:
This photograph was taken near to Wapping Police Station. It illustrates that the dockland roads were sometimes very narrow and congested, as well as being very busy in daytime.

Pass by St. John's Wharf, where photograph No.21 was taken.

Notes on photograph No.21 :
   Close to where Wapping Lane joins Wapping High Street,
stood this warehouse, being part of St. John's Wharf. Nearby was
a brewery, and this is where they kept their horses. The
ventilated hay loft was behind the arched window.

Pass by, or enter the Captain Kidd pub and, looking at photograph
No.22, visualise this busy roadside scene, one that was in operation
every weekday at most warehouses in the 1950s and 1960s. The
photograph was taken very near to where Execution Dock once stood,
by Swan Wharf. Gallows were moved here from St. Katherine's in
Elizabethan days. Pirates, sea rovers and other nautical malefactors
were hanged, tied to the river bed to be covered by three tides, tarred
for preservation, and dangled from gibbets positioned in prominent
places on the riverbank - to discourage those with villainous intent. In
the background of a Hogarth print (The IDLE 'PRENTICE turn'd away
and sent to sea, 1747), one of these tarred bodies is seen dangling from
gallows on the Millwall bank of the Isle of Dogs.

Notes on photograph No.22:
   Sights such as this one were common throughout dockland,
and would have warranted scant notice at the time. The quartet
of crane operator, foreman and two warehousemen were
handling bags of coffee beans. The soft lines of manila rope and
the taut one of steel cable, lead the eye aloft, yet allow it to dwell
on the areas of human interest.

There was another medieval tidal mill and pond somewhere just about
here. At Woods River Services pier, King Henry's Stairs, you look up
the alleyway typical of those leading to stairs on the working river. The
passageways are redolent of days past when such arteries to the water
must have been crowded with customers and shouting watermen.

Notes on photograph No.23:

The ingredients are all here in this photograph of King Henry's Stairs - the high warehouse walls on either side, gas lamp, bollards representing cannon and cannonball, and the Art Nouveau Stepney Borough Council lamp post (dated 1908). Across the road is probably a real cannon and cannonball bollard.

Now, looking onward to the bend of Gun Wharves, past King Henry's Wharves and Gun House, imagine one of the major lost features of this dockland of change, namely the many catwalks traversing the road for people and goods to reach inland warehouses from riverside wharfage (photograph No.24). We have seen but two. There were many. At night they were at their most dramatic - criss-crossing the skyline. In darkness the area was almost deserted, with only the noise of clanking barges and rattling chains to break the silence. And when there was a dense and smelly pea-soup fog shrouding the river and its surroundings, even those sounds hardly broke through the gloom. It was then that docklands were at their most dramatic and mysterious.

Notes on photograph No.24:

With a need for people or goods to be moved across the road from wharfage to warehouse, the catwalks gave this dockland road special distinction. The driver here was waiting to untie the tarpaulin and uncover his load for dockers to handle the cargo - when they had finished their dinner break.

You have not quite reached Wapping Underground Station, seen in front and on the right. Retrace your steps if you feel that you have absorbed enough of this part of historic dockland, or use the tube to return to the District Line (changing at Whitechapel) if you have walked far enough for one day (1 1/2 miles or 2.4 km). Or, you could take a No.100 bus, leaving every 15 minutes from immediately outside the Underground Station, to Aldgate, Tower Hill or Liverpool Street. All services are curtailed at week-ends.

For another detour, turn left up WAPPING LANE between Gun Place and The Carronade. You will find shops here, besides the White Swan and Cuckoo and Three Swedish Crowns pubs on the right and the Turner's Old Star pub on your left. Then cross the bridge where ships moved from Eastern Dock of London Dock on the right, through Tobacco Dock on the left and on to Western Dock. See the beautifully preserved Victorian warehouse interior (especially below ground level) of Tobacco Dock.

St. George's-in-the-East church, where Captain Bligh and his family attended, is nearby.

Return to WAPPING HIGH STREET and turn left by Wapping Underground Station. At this point, trains cross beneath the river through a tunnel that was the world's first of its type. Designed by the older Brunel in the 1820s, and using a new form of tunnelling device, it took almost 20 years to complete.

Carry on along the road and, pushing open the iron gate on the right, when it is unlocked in daytime, take the RIVERSIDE WALKWAY and THAMES PATH by St. Hilda's Wharf (photograph No.25) for another riverside view of Canary Wharf and St. Anne's, Limehouse.

St. Anne's has an interesting history. In 1711, the House of Commons granted money to Queen Anne to build 50 new churches, possibly to commemorate Marlborough's victories on the continent. Eleven were built (funded by a tax on coal coming into London by river), one being St. Anne's. The church was designed by Nicholas Hawksmoor, a pupil of Wren and Vanbrugh. Completed in 1724, its interior was totally gutted by fire in 1850. Soon refurbished, it has remained a major feature of the river landscape. You have already seen one of the other powerful and distinctive-looking Hawksmoor churches, St. George's-in-the-East.

Notes on photograph No.25:

We have now left the Upper Pool and reached the Lower Pool at St. Hilda's and Prior's Wharf. The tide is high, and the laden barges are either tied securely or about to be moved.

The most distinctive landmark in this part of dockland was the no-longer-existing "year high" chimney stack of Stepney Power Station. It was so called as there was a foot of height for each of the 365 days in the year. Just behind it and to the left is St. Anne's, Limehouse - a guide mark for shipping before the chimney was built.

The river now bends to the right around Surrey Commercial Docks, passing Bellamy's, Lower King and Queen's, and Globe Wharves.

This riverside walk will lead you back to where Wapping High Street becomes NEW CRANE PLACE at New Crane Stairs. Walk on. Photograph No.26 shows foundations being created where the St. Hilda's Wharf building now stands.

Notes on photograph No.26:

This is simply a photograph of a new river wall and of construction materials, some partly framing the spire of St. Mary's, Rotherhithe on the far side of the river.

Now, instead of taking the right turn to follow the river along WAPPING WALL, go straight ahead up GARNET STREET. On the right, and now demolished, were there is now a stepped terrace of small houses, stood two alleyways of tenement houses (Photograph No.27). They were typical examples of post war domestic squalor and poverty.

Notes on photograph No.27:

The houses were already falling into a state of dilapidation, though one proud resident had whitewashed the window surrounds to help admit more light from the dark alleyway. Coal is being sorted. The yard made a great playground for children - safe from road traffic. Locally, they were known as "honeymoon cottages", and were used for early episodes of Alf Garnett's comedy TV series (appropriately off Garnet Street).

Continue to the fine bascule (counterweighted) bridge, and from photograph Nos.28-31 imagine the bustle of this busy crossing. Yet all came to a standstill when shipping passed from the river and Shadwell Basin on the right to the Eastern Dock of London Dock on the left. This may be your first view of St. Paul's church, Shadwell, over to the right. It was built in 1820, yet the crypt is much older (1656). The church is famous for having Captain Cook as a parishioner. His son was baptised there, also Thomas Jefferson's mother, Jane Randolph. Its connections have always been maritime ones, with many sea captains buried in the churchyard.

Notes on photograph Nos.28-31:
Photograph No.28.

Behind the protective mesh is the Shadwell Basin of London Dock, seen from the bascule bridge in Garnet Street. The crossing wire and the inability of the primitive lens in my Baby Brownie camera to cope with the mesh itself, add much interest to the foreground pattern. To the right is Benson Quay, and to the left, Maynards Quay. Then, in front of St. Paul's church and the tall block of Gordon House, stands Newlands Quay on dockside previously supporting 27 and 28 warehouses and their cranes.

Photograph No.29.

An old Dutch coaster with wooden bridge (just visible in this hazy photograph) crosses from Shadwell Basin to Eastern Dock in London Dock, with the bascule bridge raised. Part of the bridge's counterweight section can be seen above.

Photograph No.30.

Looking through the wire mesh at the side of the bascule bridge in Garnet Street, the floating steam crane "Hercules" is seen being towed from Shadwell Basin to Eastern Dock of London Dock by the unseen tug, Dollar Bay.

In the background, the tall block of Gordon House, at the top of Glamis Road, is under construction. In front of it can be seen the handsome spire of St. Paul's church.

Photograph No.31.
Traffic has been stopped, and the bascule bridge in Garnet Street, with its planking pavement visible, has been raised to allow a ship to pass between Shadwell Basin and Eastern Dock of London Dock. The wall of Eastern Dock, a lock gate, and warehouse 11 are visible. Maynards Quay housing has replaced Warehouse 11. Behind the dock wall to the left is Rum Close.

Beyond the bridge, at the entrance to Newlands Quay, stood Gate 13 to Shadwell Basin (photograph No.32).

Notes on photograph No.32:
The number of cranes working indicate the importance of the dock in earlier days. In the distance you can see the bascule bridge in Glamis Road (we will cross it later) raised to allow a ship into, or out of, Shadwell Basin. The lower notice at the gate displays rates of pay for additional labour. Parts of the protective dock wall remain. Newlands Quay has replaced the warehouses.

Return down Garnet Street and turn left into WAPPING WALL, passing between New Crane Wharf and Spitalfields Co-Operative Housing Association. After those come New Crane Place and Great Jubilee Wharf, Prospect Place, the still busy Metropolitan Wharf, and Pelican Wharf.

Now it may be time to sustain the inner person at the famous river pub, the Prospect of Whitby. Once the den of thieves and now of tourists, its terraced garden and balcony command a good view of the river down to St. Anne's, Limehouse, Limekiln Creek, Dundee Wharf and Canary Wharf.

On the other side of the river you will see a bascule bridge over the disused lock and dock entrance (Surrey Lock) that once led to the vast area of Surrey Commercial Docks (now mostly filled in) and the short Grand Surrey Canal. This was the site of the original Howland Dock (1661). A bleak and extensive place of enclosed water, Surrey Docks were originally used for fish and whale blubber from Greenland but then mainly for the import and distribution of timber from the Baltic, Canada and elsewhere. Here, "rafters" formed long rafts of logs in the dock water. These they then transported to their destinations on river tides - with the help of a rowing boat. The rafters were adept at walking around on these logs in the dock and on the river, and never falling into the water.

Surrey Docks were, for me, the place of a 'minor miracle'. This is what occurred: Toward the end of the working life of these docks, wine was imported to some warehouses and storage tanks there. Most came in those days from France. I had imported a quarter cask of modest wine, having selected it at Bégadan in Bas-Médoc. It was a comparatively small cask, and had to travel aboard ship with much larger, heavier ones. As a painter of marine matters I had free access to all docks. So I arranged to visit the warehouse, test the wine in my cask, pay duty and have it transported home for bottling. But on eventually discovering it among many others, I was dismayed to find that it was only half full - the other half having leaked out aboard ship from a break in one of its staves. So I arranged to return to collect it later, being very upset to learn that I would have to pay duty as though it was full. On returning, it was a miraculous surprise to discover a patch over the break, and the cask full. It was excellent wine that I was able to bottle. With fine corks from Rankins, the nectar was savoured over many years.

Refreshed, return to our walk, looking across the road to a large red brick building, being Wapping Hydraulic Power Station. This amazing late Victorian (1890) enterprise provided hydraulic power, through a most extensive network of underground pipes, for cranes and lifts throughout the docks and much of London. The lift in a block of Edwardian flats in Victoria (several miles away), where my family lived during the 1939-1945 war, was silently powered by it.

For a short detour, take the THAMES PATH between the side of the pub and Trafalgar Court. Here you will see a bit more of the river and some stairs leading down to the shore. The path will return you to just up the road from where you set out, by the disused bascule bridge over the Shadwell Entrance to London Dock.

On the same side of the road as the Power Station, you will see the sign "Brussels Wharf • Shadwell Basin". Enter to view Shadwell Basin (photograph No.33).

Notes on photograph No.33:

These old cranes, worked by power produced by the London Hydraulic Company's Pumping Station nearby, were the first to be demolished for scrap at Shadwell Basin (quite near to where you are standing). In the photograph, the iron structure of one frames the others.

Cross the bascule bridge into GLAMIS ROAD, and immediately turn right into the THAMES PATH alleyway to King Edward VII Memorial Park. This recreational area was laid out in 1921-1922 on the site of Shadwell Fish Market and a district of insalubrious reputation. Look back for photograph No.34 and forward for No.35.

By the river and the THAMES PATH you will notice the round, brick ventilation shaft for the under-Thames Rotherhithe road tunnel.

Notes on photograph Nos.34 and 35:
Photograph No.34.

This narrow alleyway, leading back from King Edward VII Memorial Park to Glamis Road, shows old hydraulic cranes being demolished, a more modern one in use, and St. Paul's church. The figure gives scale to the entire photograph.

Photograph No.35.

King Edward VII Memorial Park was also known as Shadwell Park. It provided, and still does, one of the finest views of the river. It has always been a resting place for pensioners and, at one time, dockers. The cranes are on Free Trade Wharf. The 365' high chimney of Stepney Power Station in the distance no longer exists.

On the river in front of King Edward VII Memorial Park were the

Charrington's Barge Roads. Here, many barges were tied to tiers, awaiting lightermen and their duties. A roadsman was in charge, seeing to his various tasks by day from a hut aboard one of the barges. His job was not only to look after the barges tied to the tiers but to pick up lightermen from the shore first thing in the morning and row them out to the roads (photograph No.36). Tiers are still to be seen in the river off the park.

Sir Martin Frobisher, Elizabethan disciplinarian, explorer, buccaneer and naval (Armada) hero, sailed from a wharf near to King Edward VII Memorial Park.

Notes on photograph No.36:

Here is the roadsman for Charrington's Barge Roads rowing ashore toward Free Trade Wharf after a day's work. The tall Stepney Power Station chimney stack in the hazy distance belches noxious smoke. A few pigeons fly over on their way to roost. This photograph is very evocative of a still, misty evening on the working river.

Take the THAMES PATH in front of the flats of Free Trade Wharf. The wharfage here was always a very busy one, dealing with cargoes from the north of England and the continent. "Free Trade" referred to the repeal of certain duties in the 18th century or, more romantically, a wharf free of duties granted to Dutch sea-traders who had been brave enough to supply London during the time of the Great Plague. Look at the elegant pair of 1870 warehouses leading from the main gateway (dated 1796) to their asymmetrical river frontage.

Pass through the three-arched gateway and turn right into the busy HIGHWAY (once a very rough area frequented by sailors and now very noisy with motor traffic), maintaining the same downstream direction past Scotia Building and Atlantic Wharf. In front of you stands the entrance to the Limehouse Link tunnel and, just to the left of it, a red brick and pink stone ramp leading down to the Rotherhithe road tunnel.

Turn right into the THAMES PATH and NARROW STREET, past Ratcliffe Wharf and Commercial Wharf. On the right you will come to

Sun Wharf where Sir David Lean, a successful film director, built a house and lovely garden behind what appear to be warehouse walls. Take the alleyway next to it to just get a glimpse of part of the garden from the river bank (if you stretch right out and risk your life). Also from here you will obtain a closer view of Canary Wharf and the entrance to Limehouse Basin (photograph Nos.37-39). Go back to NARROW STREET and continue walking past Old Sun Wharf and Chinnocks Wharf.

Notes on photograph Nos. 37-39:
Photograph No.37.

Taken from off Sun, Crown Mill and London Wharves, this shows the rubbish tipping ramps at Old Sun, Chinnock's and Grand Union Wharves. Here Stepney Borough Council workers tipped refuse into barges to be towed downriver for use as infill. The festoons of manila rope and ground mooring chains give this view a theatrical look. But it was a smelly and dirty place to be.

Photograph No.38.

Still off Old Sun Wharf, this photograph of a gap between barges at rest, gives an idea of their great and simple lines.

Photograph No.39.

Taken from the same area of river bed, this shows that not all barges were of the same design, nor were they in the same state of repair. Many were the worse for wear after a lifetime of bumping into wharves, quays, tugs, ships, docks, locks and each other. This was not an unusual occurrence when considering that a barge of under 50 tons could be driven on river tides and then moored by a single lighterman with only a 25' oar, or paddle, for propulsion. Sometimes one could see a dumb lighter (untowed barge) taken from one side of a dock to the other by a lighterman holding out the sides of his jacket to act as a sail. These men were extremely handy with lines (ropes). They could curl them up and cast accurately to a pin or bollard from 25' or more away.

Nearing the entrance to Limehouse Basin, look down the road to the left, which was once Ratcliffe Highway, then The Highway, and now HORSEFERRY ROAD (photograph No.40), to see what was, to our present way of thinking, an infamous, short stretch of once cobbled pavement.

Notes on Photograph No.40:

Here men stood when hoping for work as dock labour. As they waited for what was known as "calling on" or "bomping on", they sharpened their knives on the sandstone coping stones (see the scalloped indentations). The foreman called the workers "off the stones" (the cobbled pavement) to book them in for a day's work. The men might be employed at his whim, or sometimes he would toss up as many "tallies" (work tokens) as the number of men needed. Then there would be a mighty scramble and, like animals, a fight for work. Some forms of engaging labour in this way were still practiced when I took this photograph of a bowler hatted figure approaching from behind a lamp post.

No women dock workers were employed. The tasks were considered to be too arduous for them. And the sanitary conditions were often appallingly primitive. Moreover, jobs in the industry tended, literally, to go from father to son. The two Unions, "Blues" and "Whites", co-existed with some tension, and were extremely powerful.

Coloured people were thin on the ground. "See a black man, don't swaller, hold yer collar!"

The cranes and warehouses seen in the photograph were inside Regent's Canal Dock (now Limehouse Basin). The houses in the distance were in Commercial Road.

If you would like another short detour, take HORSEFERRY ROAD and turn right into BRANCH ROAD. Shortly, on the right, you will find the dock opening where photograph No.41 was taken.

Notes on photograph No.41:

St. Anne's, Limehouse, stands framed within the legs of a fixed crane in Regent's Canal Dock.

This dock handled coal, timber and, as seen in the photograph, general cargo. Technically considered to be the mouth of the Regent's Canal, much of the cargo here was off-loaded into canal barges for transportation north on inland waterways.

Return to NARROW STREET with the Barley Mow pub (formerly the Dockmaster's House) almost in front of you (Photograph No.42). Walk as near to the river as possible. Then possibly refresh yourself.

Notes on photograph No. 42:

A Knight's tug approaches the entrance to Regent's Canal Dock (now Limehouse Basin) to move a laden barge from the knuckle. The tide is turning, and the barges are jostling at King and Queen Tier on the bend of the river beyond.

The sheds of Lavender Dock, in Surrey Commercial Docks, can be seen across the river. Beyond the timber sheds rises a gas holder of the South East Gas Board. It is a bleak day.

Return to NARROW STREET and cross the swing bridge over the entrance to Limehouse Basin. Look immediately to your left toward the Basin itself (photograph Nos.43 and 44). Once having a large lock entrance (look for the signs of it), there is now a much smaller one. Where once commercial shipping clogged the quays, now pleasure craft await their owners.

Notes on photograph Nos. 43 and 44:
Photograph No.43.

The modern cranes, like the one in the foreground, were taking over from the older variety beyond. Like many of the photographs, this one was to do with shapes and mass.

Photograph No.44.

Tackle was needed to repair the dock entrance to Regent's Canal Dock. As I was watching this, a large piece of greenheart timber was extracted from the depths. It was still in excellent condition after many years beneath the water. I considered acquiring it for sculpture, but was warned not to, because of its poisonous splinters.

It was always surprising to see such large craft in what appeared to be a small dock. The lock could take vessels up to 350' (106m) long. The Dutch ship and barge give an idea about how cluttered and busy the dock could be.

Cross the swing bridge to pass Victoria Wharf on the right. Now comes what remains of an iron bridge over Limehouse Cut. The Cut was a canal (opened in 1770) that ran from here to the Lea, a river that flows into the Thames beyond the oxbow of the Isle of Dogs. Barge traffic, bringing grain, malt, and other agricultural produce downriver from Hertfordshire, could use this waterway to save the long and more dangerous voyage past Island Gardens and Greenwich. The Cut is now joined to Limehouse Basin. A feature of this district was a row of cottages beside the sometimes deadly Victoria Lock, or Limehouse Lock (photograph Nos.45-47).

Photograph Nos.45-47:
Photograph No.45.

Barge hands and lock keepers lived in this row of cottages beside the Limehouse Lock and Cut entrance. Beyond is Northey Street, its iron bridge over the Cut, and the Regent's Canal Dock. There was always plenty of activity to be seen outside these front doors. And although children were kept in a wired enclosure for their safety, several had lost their lives over the years by falling into the water when trying to climb over the heavy beams that kept the lock walls apart. The photograph illustrates the constant struggle for cleanliness in a world of dirt (the waste paper and paperboard mills being close, too).

Photograph No.46.

Even in the post war years, this lock between the Cut and the Thames had an antiquated look about it. But there was a certain fascination in watching it being operated. The chains made a great rattling noise as the gates were opened or closed. This photograph of chain tracery, mooring pin and sluice operating wheel, caught in sunlight on a background of hefty timbers, gives a good idea of the lock's primitive strength and the visual pleasures it offered.

Photograph No.47.

Here, in the lock between the Cut and the river, water is seeping from the Cut through the gate, and falling over the cill into the lock. The gate to the river is open. The tide is low. The jetsam in the lock water is a reminder that the river was then covered with floating timber of all sorts - some of it going into the construction of my house by Limekiln Creek. Much of the floating wood was "dunnage". This was loose timber used for load-bearing divisions on which cargo rested.

From the Cut bridge look downriver to where Papermill Wharf now stands (photograph No.48) and toward the Surrey shore, the old entrance to Lavender Dock and Cucknold's Point. This point, also known as Cuckold's Point, was named, supposedly, when King John, discovered in a tavern with the wife of a miller, was obliged to pay off the aggrieved husband with a stretch of the foreshore.

Notes on Photograph No.48:

This is the corner of Hough's paper warehouse at the eastern knuckle of Limehouse Cut entrance. Hough's Wharf handled paper waste and finished products from the Limehouse Paperboard Works across the road in Narrow Street. As you may imagine, the area was rather dirty. The Temar coaster's stern is visible.

*Across the river is a mobile crane working a barge at its
wharf. Behind it stands a tall chimney stack of Enthoven Lead
Mills. On the shore are Southwark Council's rubbish tips where
Bermondsey refuse was discharged into barges for infill
downriver. The L.C.C. (London County Council) Fire Station
tower comes next, then Cucknold's Point.*

Immediately to both right and left in NARROW STREET stood
Hough's Paper Mill, Wharf and warehouses. On the river side to the
right, openings spilled smelly paper waste and rags. From the left came
the dank smell of wet paper and the noise of grinding wheels. It was not
a pleasant spot. The landscape down Narrow Street was dominated by
the enormous chimney (photograph No.49) .

Notes on photograph No.49:

*The Stepney Power Station's 365' tall chimney stack pours out
smoke. Steam rises from near ground level. It is raining, and the
lorry delivering waste paper to a warehouse of the Limehouse
Paperboard Works on the left is partly covered by a tarpaulin.*

*The aspect is bleak, cold and wet. So a warming drink at The
Grapes (formerly The Bunch of Grapes) around the corner would
have been of prime concern to the photographer.*

Keeping to NARROW STREET, with Blyth's Wharf on the right
and where the Stepney Power Station stood on the left, we reach
another famous river pub, The Grapes. We are now in Limehouse and
the area from which Charles Dickens drew so much inspiration. It is
thought that he spent time in The Grapes ("The Six Jolly Fellowship
Porters") when writing so clearly about the district in "Our Mutual
Friend". Limehouse also appears in his "Dombey and Son", "The
Uncommercial Traveller" and "Great Expectations".

Look over to The House They Left Behind pub (formerly the Black
Lion) on the left in Ropemakers' Fields, and right at a row of houses
favoured at one time or other by journalists, publishers, doctors,

politicians and television people. Then pass (or enter) Booty's Riverside Bar, and you will come to Woodward Fisher's Yard (Spark's Wharf) at Duke's Shore Stairs (photograph Nos.50 and 51). On January 11th 1660, Samuel Pepys reached here having walked across the Isle of Dogs. He had taken a barge to Blackwall where a new ship, the Royal Oake, was about to be launched. It was clearly cold, as before he set out on this return journey, he had "taken a cup of burnt wine at the taverns". And, no doubt, he stopped off to view the ropeyards at Ropemakers' Fields to check on the quality of ropes being made there for the Navy.

Notes on photograph Nos.50 and 51:
Photograph No.50.

A police launch passes upstream in front of Duke's Shore Stairs. On the other side of the river are the Southwark Council's tips with barges (one on the campshed). To the left is the L.C.C. Fire Station and some of Gazelee's barges. H.V. Enthoven's lead works chimney is to the right.

The weighted cradle in the foreground (they were called "stocks", "barge chocks" or, if three or four together, a "grid iron") would be anchored down beneath a floating barge so that its hull could be repaired at low tide.

Photograph No.51

These men are repairing the "after swim" of a barge on the shore off Spark's Yard at Duke Shore Stairs and Wharf, near Dunbar Wharf (where a Japanese, Admiral Count Heihachiro Togo, once worked as a shipwright when learning naval science in England).

Pass the offices of E.W. Taylor Group of Companies (owners of Dunbar Wharf). Across the road, where the Limehouse Link road runs underground, once stood Limehouse Brewery, famous in its day for brewing beer for export (India Pale Ale - IPA). Duncan Dunbar made his fortune at Dunbar Wharf (on the right) by exporting this ale in the 1830s and 1840s (photograph Nos.52 and 53).

Take the RIVERSIDE WALKWAY through the buildings of Duke Shore Wharf to gain the river side of Dunbar Wharf. See the suspended bridge over Limekiln Creek, Dundee Wharf and on downriver to the sloping Cascades building. Look upstream to Free Trade Wharf and beyond. The views are magnificent. Then return right away to NARROW STREET.

As another possible diversion (a longer one), the path and foot bridge leading from a tubular gateway to the left would take you across open ground to Limehouse Basin, the Regent's Canal and then along its towpath for a 1 1/2 mile (2.4 km) walk to the Ragged School Museum (open on Wednesdays and Thursdays 10.00am - 5.00pm and first Sunday of the month 2.00 -5.00pm. Admission free). The museum, housed in 1872 canal warehouses at 46-48 Copperfield Road, commemorates Dr. Barnado and tells the story of East End people through the ordinary objects of work and leisure.

Notes on photograph Nos.52 and 53:
Photograph No.52.

This view from Dunbar Wharf looks up Limekiln Creek to the studio house I built there in 1965 on the site of Passmore's offices. Dundee Wharf and its offices are on the right. St. Dunstan's Wharf, where hay, in earlier times, was unloaded from barges and supplied to the Royal Mews, is one of the wharfside warehouses on the left behind the rest of Dunbar Wharf. Cargoes handled here were of a general nature, but these bags of chopped coconut, casks of orange and blackcurrant juice, raw fruits and ginger were regulars. The casks seen here held juices and ginger.

Photograph No.53.

These rolls of paper in strops (loops of spliced rope) lie on Dunbar Wharf. The barges rest on the mud of Limekiln Creek. The flotsam and jetsam lying on the mud of the creek at low tide was a regular feature when the wind had come from a southerly direction. Even though some pretty nasty things floated up the creek, one could not help but inspect it - from a distance.

On the road again, and past Dunbar Wharf, notice St. Anne's, Limehouse, over to the left. As you approach the crossroads at the end of NARROW STREET, look at the ornamental front of St. Dunstan's Wharf on the right (from where hay was distributed, piled high on horse-drawn carts) and the old warehouses to the right of it where sacks of juniper berries from Italy (for the making of London gin) once scented the air around.

You now come to the junction of NARROW STREET, THREE COLT STREET and, ahead, LIMEHOUSE CAUSEWAY, the notorious and very narrow street of the past that was known for prostitution, opium dens and Puckapoo Chinese gambling (photograph Nos.54 and 55). The warehouse on the corner was where "Uncle" stored bananas from floor to roof. The fruit was ripened by a single gas ring.

Notes on photograph Nos.54 and 55:
Photograph No.54.

Looking back from the junction of Three Colt Street, where Narrow Street becomes Limehouse Causeway, the Barley Mow Estate was dwarfed by the chimney stack of Stepney Power Station. The tower block had just been constructed from prefabricated sections and was not yet occupied.

Photograph No.55.

The Barley Mow Estate was under construction, and its rough-cast prefabricated sections had just been put together. Three Colt Street leads away to the left from the palings on the right of the photograph, past Bernie's Cafe, the Five Bells and Bladebone pub, and on to St. Anne's, Limehouse, seen here with its tower bathed in river mist. Dockers lived in the Council block to the right.

Turn right into THREE COLT STREET, past the banana warehouse and my studios with its garage where much wine was bottled, and then right again into Limekiln Wharf (photograph Nos.56 and 57). It was here that lime kilns were established in medieval times. The name Limehouse may be derived from the lime "oasts", another name for kilns. Look back and forward in eye and mind.

Notes on photograph Nos.56 and 57:
Photograph No.56.

This is the view from the studio house I built with Max Jarnot in Three Colt Street.

In front is Limekiln Creek leading to the Thames. It is high tide. On the right is St. Dunstan's Wharf, with a barge moored at Dunbar Wharf beyond. The high-fly crane in the centre measured 60' with a jib of 120'. It, with a smaller mobile crane, served Dunbar Wharf.

In the distance, on the far bank, are the lead mills, known as "lead pots", with their two "melting chimneys".

To the left is Limekiln Wharf, where once chalk boats and colliers tied up to supply the lime kilns. Beyond is Dundee Wharf with its massive, fortress-like warehouse.

The Lockett Wilson coaster at Dundee Wharf, with prow, masts and bridge just visible, plied its trade between London, on the Thames, and Paris, on the Seine.

This fascinating view was ever-changing. Tides, flotsam and jetsam, water, mud, the odd body or part of one, a rat or two, barges, ships, dock activity, river traffic, the thumping and crashing of ships and barges at night and day... All this and much more made it a most wonderful place in which to live and work.

The photograph was taken through a piece of netting when dock work had finished for the day and at the turn of the tide after north-easterly winds. The view encompasses most of the major elements of dockland riverscape.

Photograph No.57.

We look back at my studio house toward the end of 1965. To the right are Dundee, Limekiln and Limehouse Wharves. Ropes, timber and a crane on rails can be seen.

The name of Service and Luton Wharf was no longer used for my dock wall, where once, in much earlier times, stagnated "the black ditch". On the left, Dunbar Wharf led to St. Dunstan's Wharf and Wilson's Ship Store.

The vessel, that for many years lay rotting at the wharf on the left, was an unused Customs Survey Unit boat. The refuse lying on the mud of the creek represents a typical collection seen at low tide after a blow from a south-westerly wind.

We have now come to the end of our walk through this important part of London's dockland. I do hope that you have enjoyed it, savoured the present, obtained a feel for its past, and imagined the future.

There are some who might see this guide as an investigation into dockland pubs. There is no shortage of them (14), dock work in the past being such a thirsty job. Start at the Dickens Inn, St. Katherine Dock. After Hermitage Basin come the Scots Arms and China Ship, followed by the Town of Ramsgate. Near to that old one is the Captain Kidd. Into Wapping Lane (one of the diversions) you will find the White Swan and Cuckoo, the Three Swedish Crowns and Turner's Old Star. In Wapping Wall, and on the right, is the famous Prospect of Whitby. Now, some way off, are the Grapes, of Dickens renown, the House They Left Behind, and Booty's. After turning right into Three Colt Street, the Enterprise is around the corner beyond Limekiln Wharf. And lastly, should you decide to return by bus from Commercial Road, by St. Anne's, Limehouse, there is the Five Bells and Bladebone in Three Colt Street for a final swig.

ONWARD

Possibly continue down the side of Limekiln Dock to rejoin the Thames Path. Perhaps return to Limehouse Causeway, turning right into it to take the Docklands Light Railway nearby at Westferry. Either take a train from there back to Tower Gateway or Bank, or on to Island Gardens and cross to Greenwich by the pedestrian tunnel (known as "the pipe"). From the pier in Greenwich take a pleasure boat back to the Tower or Westminster (your all-day pass will not cover the cost of this river trip). Alternatively, walk down Three Colt Street, past the Five Bells and Bladebone (an old-fashioned and mellow dockland pub), past St. Anne's and turn left into roguish Commercial Road to catch a No.15 bus. Or cut across the churchyard to the bus stop, looking to the left at the mysterious and elegant pyramid, erected by Hawksmoor at the same time as the church. The No.15 bus will take you back to Aldgate, the Tower of London, Lower Thames Street, the Monument, Cannon Street Station, St. Paul's Cathedral, City Thameslink Station, Fleet Street, Aldwich, Strand, Charing Cross Station, Trafalgar Square, Piccadilly Circus, Regent Street, Oxford Circus and on to Marble Arch and Paddington - depending on the destination displayed on the front of the bus.

Of course, you *could* do it all in reverse.

THE
PHOTOGRAPHS
1-57

1

2

3

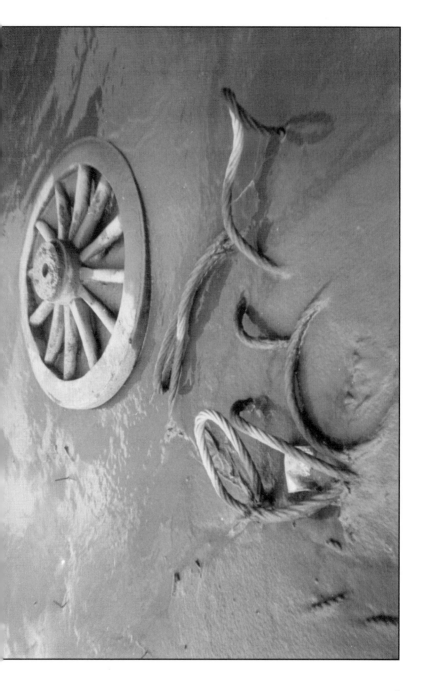

4

5

6

7

8

9

10

11

12

13

14

16

17

21

22

23

24

25

26

27

28

29

30

31

33

34

35

36

37

38

39

40

41

42

43

44

45

46

47

48

49

50

51

52

54

56

THE
MAPS
1-4

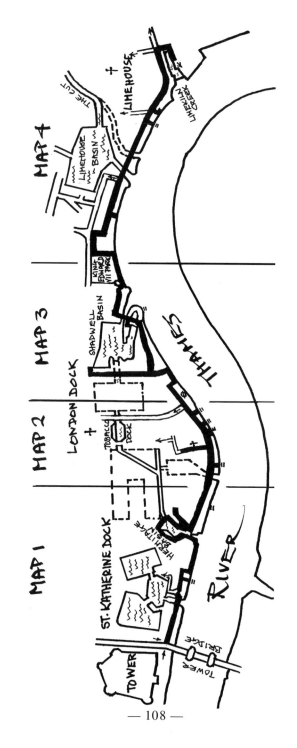

MAP 1 MAP 2 MAP 3 MAP 4

ST. KATHERINE DOCK
LONDON DOCK
SHADWELL BASIN
LIMEHOUSE BASIN

TOWER
TOWER BRIDGE
HERMITAGE BASIN
TOBACCO DOCK
KING EDWARD VII PARK
LIMEHOUSE
THE CUT
LIMEHOUSE
LIMEKILN CREEK

RIVER
THAMES

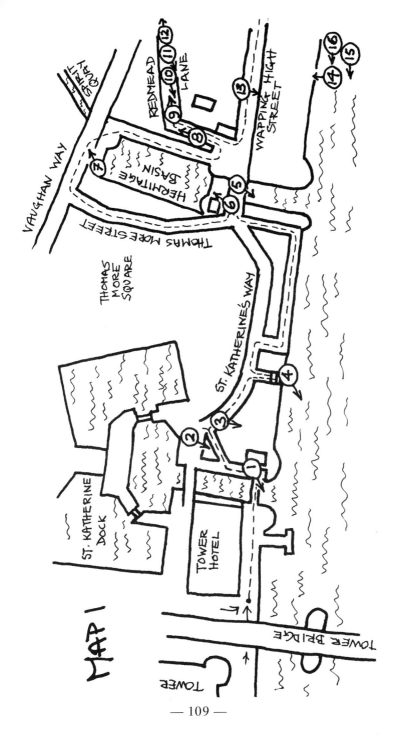

MAP 1

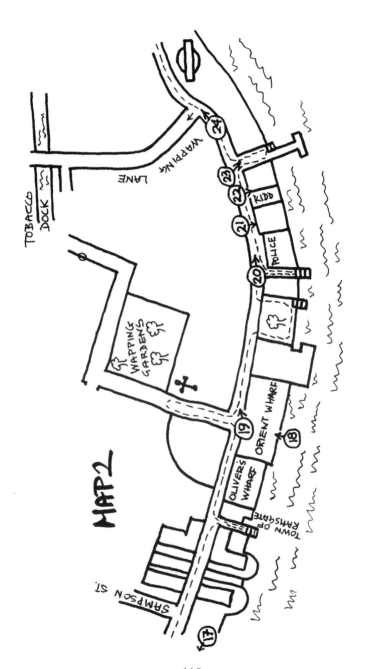

MAP 2

SAMPSON ST

TOWN OF RAMSGATE

OLIVER'S WHARF

ORIENT WHARF

WAPPING GARDENS

TOBACCO DOCK

WAPPING LANE

KIDD

POLICE

17
18
19
20
21
22
23
24

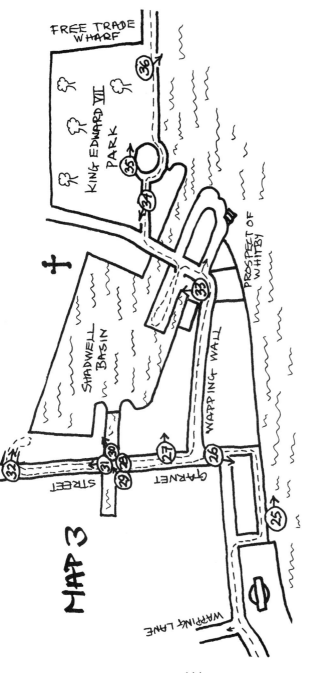

MAP 3

FREE TRADE WHARF

KING EDWARD VII PARK

SHADWELL BASIN

PROSPECT OF WHITBY

WAPPING WALL

GARNET STREET

WAPPING LANE

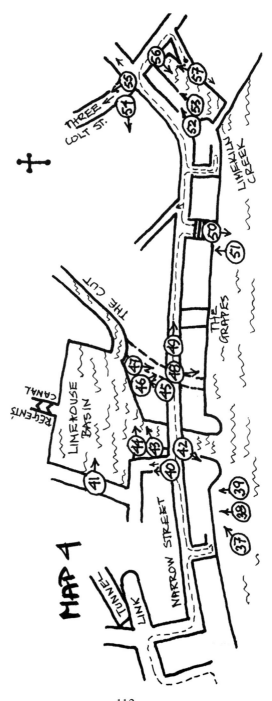

MAP 4

INDEX

BIBLIOGRAPHY

History of the Port of London (volumes 1&2), Sir J.G. Broodbank, Daniel O'Connor, 1921.

Port of London, D.J. Owen, Port of London Authority, 1927.

Peepshow of the Port of London, A.G. Linney, Sampson Low, Marston & Co., 1930.

Limehouse Through Five Centuries, J.G. Birch, The Sheldon Press, 1930.

The Port of London (pamphlet), Port of London Authority, 1966.

London's Lost Riverscape, edited by Chris Ellmers and Alex Werner, Viking, 1988.

Docklands Heritage, London Docklands Development Corporation, 1987.

Ben's Limehouse, B. Thomas, Ragged School Books, 1987.

On the River, Pam Schweitzer and Charles Wegner, Age Exchange, 1989.

Judge Jeffreys, Madge Darby, Connor & Butler, 1989.

Captain Bligh in Wapping, Madge Darby, History of Wapping Trust, 1990.